44839:
Poetry from a Zip Code

Volume III
2019

44839: Poetry from a Zip Code

Volume III
2019

Edited by Rob Smith

Drinian Press LLC

44839: *Poetry from a Zip Code*
Volume III, 2019
Editor: Smith, Rob (1947-)
©2020 Robert Bruce Smith, Jr

All rights for the individual poems in this volume remain the sole property of the poets. Rights for inclusion in this volume have been obtained.

Cover photo: Egret at Lakefront Park, Huron, OH
Photo credit: Rob Smith
Cover design: Drinian Press LLC

Drinian Press LLC
PO Box 63
Huron, Ohio 44839

Online at www.DrinianPress.com

Acknowledgements: Mila Kette's "Two Wooden Bowls" was previously published in *Heartlands Today* (Fireland's Writing Center, 2002) and in *The Best of Heartlands: 1991-2005* (Firelands Writing Center). Her poem, "Lil' Boat and Sky" appeared in *Heartlands 2003*. Bruce Molnar's "*Migizi Yabwen* Eagle Dreamer" was published in *Pokégnek Yajdanawa*, (*Démen gises* 2017) the newsletter of the Pokagon Band of the Potawatomi Nation. Rob Smith's "Sister" first appeared in *The Immigrant's House* (Drinian Press, 2012). All poems used by permission of the poets.

Library of Congress Control Number: 2020934075

ISBN-13: 978-1-941929-11-7

Printed in the United States of America

Foreword

This collection of poetry was released in April of 2020 as part of the Huron Public Library's celebration of National Poetry Month. It is the third volume that has grown out of our citizens' support of poetry. The form and content of these poems vary greatly, but, whether serious or comedic, they reflect both the timelessness of the human experience and the life of our community.

The program itself is a volunteer effort, and has been offered as a model for poets living in other areas of the country. We are aware of at least one group that has adapted it as a fund-raiser for local charities. Whatever the motive, the result is nurturing expressions of the internal/emotional space of women, men, and young people.

This is grassroots poetry. At its best, it offers profound things in everyday words. It relates our experiences to the very human search for meaning. In books like this, insights are shared with neighbors. It's been over a hundred years since Robert Frost wrote:

> No tears in the writer, no tears in the reader. No surprise for the writer, no surprise for the reader. For me the initial delight is the surprise of remembering something I didn't know I knew.
>
> (From: "The Figure a Poem Makes")

His words are still true.

RBS

44839: Poetry from a Zip Code
Volume III: 2019

| Contents |

Jill Kinser   13
    First Place Award: Haiku for You
    In the Water
    The Gift

Jennie Mae Fish   16
    Second Place Award: The Immigrants
    Expectant Summer
    Mordener Kill (Creek)
    The Vegetable Boys

Donna Gassett   20
    Third Place Award: Rose in the Cradle
    So Much to Celebrate
    Take Her Hand
    I'm Committed

Gerald (Jerry) Bauer   24
    Hear the Silence
    Hope of Spring
    Silent Love
    Fall Color

Robert Paul Boehk   28
    The Wind
    The Gift

Nancy Brady   29
    In Memory of Marcella Buck
    The Unknown
    We Buried Our Friend Today
    The Witch

Eileen Wikel-Darby   34
> My Beautiful Pink Shoes
> Springtime
> April
> 44839 Country

Bill Gassett   38
> You and I Are Different
> Courage to Be Kind
> Thankful
> Contentment

Will Gravitt   42
> 404
> Jill Michelle
> Tearing Away
> just right

Gary Harmon   46
> Poems that Don't Rhyme

Joan Harris   48
> Star-spangled Elegy
> Rest Area
> How Do I Love Cheese
> Submerged

Doni Hartley   52
> Creation as Told by a Third-Grade Boy

Jerry Hartley   53
> Old Fiddle on the Shelf
> I Spy with My Little Eye
> Daylight Savings Time

Samantha Heffley   56
> My Song
> Fighting for Normalcy
> Inside the Walls

Warren Holliday   59
> Brew Time
> The Wine Glass

Mila Kette   61
              Two Wooden Bowls
                    Ebony
               Lil' Boat and Sky

Stephanie Kramer   65
                Cottage Life

Samantha Laffay   66
                  Surprises
                  Experience

William Lucht   68
               What's My Line

Don McGee   69
              On Christmas Eve
             Memorial Day Tribute

Loretta Majoy   73
                 On Sleeping
             Say No to a Fat Cat
                  For Mario

Bruce Molnar   76
         Migizi Yabwen (Eagle Dreamer)

Robert Reynolds   78
                  My Pond
             Walking in the Woods

David Rolsten   81
                    Hiker

Ronald M. Ruble   82
                  Rustlings
                 Even-Keeled
        When Innocence Flavored the Air
                  Honor Them

Joel D. Rudinger 86
    Bottle o' What
    Life is a Dance to a Song We Cannot Hear
    When Winds Blow Me
    Every Song Comes to an End

Domenic Sberna 90
    The Technological Struggle
    A Better Outlook
    Hope

Linda Simmons 93
    Come Summer

Rob Smith 94
    Kesiah
    Sister
    Keeping House
    Seasonal Inflation

Colette Sommer Steuk 99
    Frogs
    The Day is Done
    Poem

Dana Sandberg Vargo 100
    Inner Eye

Sandra Wright 101
    The Plan
    For Alex
    Summer Night

Index of Poets 104

About the Contest and the Judging 109

44839:
Poetry from a Zip Code

Volume III: 2019

Jill Kinser

Haiku for you

Dark clouds overhead
Until your sunshine broke through
Unexpectedly

In the Water

Join me in the water
Where it's cool and still and deep.
There we'll float upon our backs,
And escape all noise and heat.
As we move toward each other
Or apart, again we'll be
As we were when we were younger;
Still as peace and still carefree.
As the willows drape above us
And the dragonflies flit by,
Submerge below the surface
And we both will be baptized.
Let the water circle round us,
Let the quiet take its toll.
Come join me in the water,
Let the water save our souls.

The Gift

You reach down in the sand, then place a perfect sand dollar in
my hand.

I tell you that, even after many years visiting the beach, I had
never found a complete sand dollar on the shore.

I have found many broken pieces and have seen whole urchins in
gift shops, but I have never pulled a complete
circle from the ocean.

Now you stand here handing me this gift. And it is so like you
to give me something so beautiful and perfect
and now truly known.

The Immigrants

Jennie Mae Fish

They sit and stare
   through fences of metal,
   in human cages,
   like animals corralled
   for slaughter,

Haunted eyes wet with
   pools of waiting tears,
Mother cradling a blanket
   still scent with baby's skin,

Trembling sadness,
   echoes of children's cries,
   wrenched,
   bereft,
   ears beating
   with heart tones of loss,

The hope of America,

The promise of America,

The dream of America,

Destroyed.

Expectant Summer

A day to remember...

Sunshine slanting through
a wooden window frame,
The side yard fragrant with heaps
of just mowed grasses,
Beds of portulaca, saffron, peach, and white
planted among the tufa rock,
Our neighbor dog Brownie
smiling at the screen door,
Shouts and whoops from Karen's plastic pool,
The whole summer laid at my feet,
And then it begins...
A police car pulls into the driveway.
My mother screams at me,
"Shut the door!"
I react instinctively to her shrill command
And with all my six-year old might
SLAM the front door and run to her,
Frightened and bewildered,
How long do the men in blue
pound and shout while
I huddle and panic with my mom?
At some point they enter our home
and take my mother away in their police car,
And I know that my life is changed...Forever.

Mordener Kill (Creek)

Still waters gather,
Pool,
Press over creek grasses, stone,
Stream along banks
Lined with honeysuckle
And dipping willows,
Cascade,
Plunge!
Foamy and frothy
Into a swimming hole
Filled with summer children.

The Vegetable Boys

The vegetable boys are coming!

Sinewy arms, strong hands,

Lift and carry
baskets laden with carrots,

bunched and orange,
Tipped in feathery greens,

Beets, round and purple,
still dusted with garden dirt,

Chartreuse lettuces
with crisp curly frills,

Red and white radishes
tied with twine,

Fat ripe tomatoes
ready for salting,
still warm from the sun,

Later…crunchy salad supper.

Rose in the Cradle

Donna Gassett

There's a rose in the cradle where you should have
    been
A tiny faded bloom
And our dreams for you are laid to rest
In this quiet empty room

Little one, you left too soon for me to hold
Before you ever heard your name
Little one, you left too soon for me to hold
But not too soon for me to love.

Now the One who created your delicate form
Has welcomed you in His home
Where no baby cries or rose ever dies
And You're cradled as His own

Someday I'll hold you, know you
Call you by your name and take your hand
When we're together, together again…

Little one, you left too soon for me to hold
Before you ever heard your name
Little one, you left too soon for me to hold
But not too soon for me to love.

So Much to Celebrate

Came home from school with a smile on my face;
I had aced the test
Mama lit a candle, put the teapot on; and then she said
"Let's have a party like the time we did
When you won the race...like you hoped you would
There's so much to celebrate, celebrate."

Came home from school with a tear in my eye;
I had flunked the test
Mama lit a candle, put the teapot on; and then she said:
"Let's have a party like the time we did
When you lost the race...but you ran to win
There's so much to celebrate, celebrate."

Mama has run her final race;
We were gathered around her bed
We light a candle, kiss her good-bye; then Mama says:
"We'll have a party in my new home
Where we'll sing together around the throne;
There's so much to celebrate, celebrate."
Forever we will celebrate, celebrate

Take Her Hand

I let go today of her hand as she wobbled away on her bike
It hurt to see her fall in the sand;
That's the part that I don't like.
But how will she learn to ride if I never learn to let go;
She needs someone by her side,
And Lord, if it's You, that's all I need to know.

Take her hand, take her hand as I give it up to You
Take her hand, help her stand and lead her gently too.
Take her hand, take her hand,
I can trust her to You I know
Take her hand, take her hand, O Lord.

I let go today of her hand
As she walked down the aisle in white
To marry a special young man whose love is her delight
With joy I let her go free to build a life of her own
She was entrusted to me, but I know she's Yours, O Lord
And Yours alone.

Take her hand, take her hand as I give it up to You
Take her hand, help her stand and lead her gently too.
Take her hand, take her hand,
I can trust her to You I know
Take her hand; take her hand as I now let it go.

I'm Committed

Now that we've been married a hundred years or so
We look a little frayed around the edges
Feelings come and go like the winter snow
We can't rely on them to keep our pledges

But I'm committed,
Committed to staying faithful to you
Promises once made still hold true
Even when you fail me
When there are differences and strife
I'm committed, committed to loving you all my life

We have so much in common after all these years
Like sweet parental dreams and living nightmares
Holidays and bills, some romantic thrills
And other days of simply coasting…who cares?

For richer or for poorer we vowed in solemn tones
But I was really planning on the richer
In sickness and in health
I said the words myself
But, my, it's hard to care for him that's sicker!

But I'm committed,
Committed to staying faithful to you
Promises once made still hold true
God will never fail me and He will help me be your wife
And I'm committed, committed to loving you all my life

Hear the Silence

Gerald (Jerry) Bauer

Silence sounds in
wind in the desert,
waves crashing on seashore,
leaves rustling in trees.

Silence sounds when
no human voice speaks,
no machines make their noise.

Only the sounds of nature's earth.
God reveals
through silent sounds.
I hear God speak
unspoken words.

I hear God speak
in the sound of silence.

Hope of Spring

One bright morning
singing birds greet
blazing orange sun,
rising in the east.
Shades of red, pink, purple
in azure blue sky.
Sound of spring,
vision of spring,
hope of spring.
New day,
bright day,
singing day,
breaks open new life,
new possibilities,
new world.
God's creative work,
will it work in me
the hope of spring?

Silent Love

What does it mean
to walk in love?
Speak words or give gifts,
does it really matter?

The presence of a loved one,
no gifts or words needed.
Jesus gives His presence
continually to me.
Needs quiet and attention
for me to see.

The presence of being,
silent love.

Fall Color

Red, yellow, orange leaves,
a blaze of autumn color.
Season of the year,
season of life.
Waning days of fall,
waning years of life.

Born of color,
eternity in life.

The Wind

Robert Paul Boehk

In our lives the wind is ever stirring.
A Spring breeze sweetening the air, the fragrance
of lilacs and freshness and grandmothers.
At times though, the wind howls, whipping and tossing, unsettling us.
With the ferocity of hurricanes, the wind reveals
The awesome power of almighty God.
Confusion comes, fear and strife creep into our fragile lives.
Yet He calms us. Be still. Peace.

And the breeze warms, heated by summer's glow.
Happiness. Splashing. Laughing.
Together our family plays in the sun, cooled by the gentle breeze.
But it ever changes. Blowing, growing crisp and cool.
Warm days and frosty nights; leaves drift down.
One by one they sail as silent messengers telling of another year passing.
And childhood whispers by.

And the wind howls once more;
Colder now, it bites and steals the sun's warmth.
But we are protected, warmed by His glow.
We are safe from the wind.
We see its beauty.

Nancy Brady

In Memory of Marcella Buck
For Shirley

In memory of…
   the stone markers say
   followed by a name.

New to the area,
   I concoct my own tales.
     of who they were or what they did.

One plaque in particular was
   overshadowed by a blue spruce.
So tall,
   the tree dwarfed the buildings around it…
     until one day it was just gone,
       cut to the ground,
        only the stump remaining.

For days, weeks, months
   the stone lay bared
   to the caprices of the weather—
   to the wind and to the rain
until finally a Norway maple
   was planted where the fir once stood.
Not as majestic,
   but with leaves of aubergine, room to grow, and
flanked by day lilies of gold,
   it would shelter the plaque once more.

Then silk flowers began to appear
   throughout the year.
  Poinsettias in December,
   mums and daisies in the fall,
red roses providing color in the snow.
Until I learn the story...
   About the restaurant that once stood there
    and of the woman who sat,
      greeting customers and friends,
   day after day...

The plaque taking
  on new meaning,
   the name becoming a reality—
of a mother who's remembered
  and a daughter who never forgets.

The Unknown

On the road between two towns,
   Huron and Vermilion,
A ridge covered with white stones,
   markers,
      some old,
         some pristine and new.

It's a chosen place,
    near where a body washed ashore.

Almon Ruggles found it,
   whether surveying or walking,
a body, clothed
   in a navy blue double-breasted jacket.

The man had done his duty,
   Ruggles knew his,
Got a coffin,
   buried the stranger,
      marked the grave.
The waves and currents chose the place.

Oak Bluff Cemetery, it's called today,
    near Cranberry Creek.
Up the stairs, through the gate.

   His epitaph is short:
   UNKNOWN
   U.S. Sailor
    1813

We Buried Our Friend Today

We buried our friend today.

Although the funeral was a week ago,
  We buried our friend today.
The sun decided to shine, and
  flags snapped in the wind
    in a salute to the Marine.

After the benediction,
  there was quiet,
    the family saying their last goodbye
    to the man they all loved.

So I stood,
  in the meditative silence,
    watching red rose petals like tears drop
      one by one onto the casket.

One minute, two minutes,
  and more passed.
No one in a rush to leave,
  or speak.
As the flags continued to snap
  in the breeze.

The Witch

She's there in the cracks
  if you look
  in the front of the church
Always in the same place
  except she tries to hide.

Still, most people ignore her
  or maybe they just don't see.

Witchever it is,
  she's there.

She hides under snow
  and leaves,
Come summer, she hides beneath
  her straggly crabgrass hair,
  covered by her witch's hat.
And with the passing years,
  she hides, sinking
    deeper into the walk.

Still, I always make sure to
  never disturb her peace.
  walking around her,
    to the right or left, but
    avoiding her face.
Sometimes, I speak:
"Are you a good witch
  or a bad witch?
"Or are you an insufferable
  know-it-all like Hermione?"

She never says,
  just smiles her
    enigmatic smile.

My Beautiful Pink Shoes

Eileen Wikel Darby

Thinking back to things I wore
And fashions that made the news,
Regardless what color was in
I loved my beautiful pink shoes.

I had made a springtime dress,
A cotton print in rosy hues.
It was on the way to the grocery
I saw the beautiful pink shoes.

I knew my checkbook suffered
A case of the spending blues.
I'd have to squeeze the cash
To buy the beautiful pink shoes.

That day I was abundantly blessed
With coupons clipped from the news.
After frugally planning the menus
I bought the beautiful pink shoes.

The dress is faded, purple is in,
My checkbook still sings the blues
But up in the attic worn and loved
Kept are my beautiful pink shoes.

Springtime

I can soon forget
Winter's chill
And brown fields so dead
When I view bright blue skies
And tulip buds of red.

I can soon forget
Dark bulky clothing
And high boots
When I taste the freedom
Of open sandals
And see little maple shoots.

I can soon forget
Many brooding cares
And lay little aches aside
When green grass and balmy breezes
Lure me outside.

April

Welcome to the fragrant breeze of April
Persuading the chilly winds of March to flee,
Erasing memory of winter, dark and cold,
Showing green leaves on the maple tree.

I long to see tall red and yellow tulips,
Daffodils and lilacs, bluebirds too.
The bright sunshine cheers my heart
When springtime skies turn azure blue.

Farmers in the fields planting yellow corn,
Expecting to reap a harvest in the fall,
Hoping summer gentle rains and sunshine
Grow cornstalks firm and tall.

Stay awhile refreshing April, rush not May,
I long to retain the aroma of purple lilac,
Yet be assured a happy summer
Is not far away.

44839 Country

The city of Huron, Ohio is lovely.
Its lake enhanced beauty and pleasant parks
Promote joy and preserve history.
Huron is zip code 44839.

This code also goes beyond Huron,
Almost to Milan and Berlin Heights,
Past Mitiwanga to Beulah Beach.
No longer city, but beautiful country.

Drive out River Road, east of Huron,
Enjoy the scenery along the river.
Though it gets muddy its banks bloom
With wild flowers in late summer.

Turn on almost any road past River,
It will probably be named for a farm family
Who owned eighty acres in the 1800's,
Like Mason, Wikel, Huff, or Knight.

Here white-tailed deer travel free
Across farm fields. A red fox
May show his face as he hurries
Over the meadow and into the woods.

Springtime finds a tractor in every field;
Anxious farmers planting corn or soy beans;
Anxious because Ohio weather is unpredictable.
Around July 4th they harvest wheat

October is the time to pick corn.
The big combine does the job.
Soy beans are harvested in November
Using the same machine.

The farmer and his family welcome winter
Some travel to warmer climates,
It's then they enjoy writing back
To friends and family at zip code 44839.

Bill Gassett

You and I Are Different
To my wonderful wife

Opposites attract, they say
But acceptance keeps love strong
To all who wish their mate would change
I dedicate this song.

You and I are different in so many ways
I like golf and pizza
You like rainy days.

Accepting others' differences is sometimes hard, that's true
But I am finding deeper joy every time I do.

I've been known to talk a bit
You've been somewhat quiet.
I've been known to eat too much
But you eat a balanced diet.

I accept the way you are
The who…the what…the why
And to find that same acceptance
Is enough to make me cry.

Yes, you and I are different in so many ways
I like golf and pizza
You like rainy days.

Courage to Be Kind

Taking a stand…standing alone
When you're afraid and shaking
When you speak up for those who can't
You're a hero in the making.

Courage rises up and fights
Defends, protects, forgives
Runs and helps those at risk
That's where true courage lives.

If it were easy all would go
To serve the weak and lost
Self sacrifice is tough and rare
But always worth the cost.

To see hope and joy in their eyes
People who need TLC
Tender, Loving Care must rise
From the hearts of you and me.

Courage is more than just a word
It's a worthy way to live
Anybody can receive
The blessed are those who give.

So give to those who need your help
True Love is color blind
Reach out and lift someone in need
It takes courage to be kind.

Thankful

What does it mean to be thankful?
It means to "show and tell"
Expressing for every blessing
Songs of Praise to Emmanuel.

To acknowledge and declare
All my gifts from God above
Giving Glory and Gratitude
To the Lord of Perfect Love.

It also means thanking people
For their generosity
Thoughtful, gracious kindness
And hospitality.

To be thankful means to smile
Let Love flow from your eyes
To hug someone who blessed you
That's how Love multiplies.

Thankfulness will not be found
On just Thanksgiving Day
It's found in grateful, humble hearts
And always on display.

To be thankful means giving back
Helping those in need
Acts of random kindness
That's thankfulness indeed!

Contentment

What does it mean to be content?
It means to have enough.
It means not striving to get more
Or coveting other's stuff.

To be content means Giving Thanks
For my daily bread.
To praise the Lord for all He gives
From nail scarred hands that bled.

To be content means…I'm at peace
In every circumstance
Knowing God is in control
That I don't live by chance.

Contentment is a state of mind
That saints of old displayed
Instead of griping at sour lemons
They made sweet lemonade!

So cultivate the mind of Christ
Who taught us every grace
May God see Joy and Gratitude
In every heart and face.

404

Will Gravitt

Yes.
This will be the place.
No other will supplant it.
Many have paused to hide here.
But on this night, we find each other.

Jill Michelle

Was it the right hand or the left?
I remember it perfectly
It was dark; the lake was shimmering
The love was new, but coming from an ancient place
Our stride was slow and expectant
First, it brushed
Then, I took hold of your right hand
She smiles
It was the left.

Tearing Away

So much stitching between two fabrics
I knew both couldn't remain
I knew I was the seam
I knew there had to be a tearing away
I didn't know that everything would rip with that kind
  of pull
I didn't know that everyone would cry
I didn't know that everyone would fear
So much stitching between two fabrics

just right

"You want to watch a movie?" – just right
"You want to go to the beach?" – just right
"You want to hear about this book I read?" – just right
"You want me to play this new song I learned?" – just right
"You want me to take these off?" – just right
"You want a whiskey drink?" – just right
"You want to be with me forever?" – just right

Poems that Don't Rhyme

Gary Harmon

We've such a fine town
Our library's the best
Highlight of the year?
the annual poets contest!

Each year I enter
Hoping my works will shine
But I keep being beat out
by poems that don't rhyme!

The judges are all intellectuals
You'd think They knew better
A poem that don't rhyme
Ain't a poem- It's a letter!

Or it's an essay, a book
Or maybe a tome
But one thing it ain't
It just ain't a poem

A friend said quit bitchin'
You just gripe and yammer
You might win somthin'
if you'd use better grammer

It ain't my grammar
that keeps me at the back of the line
My work's not artsy enough they say
It's from some old distant time.

"It's so old fashioned." they tell me
"It couldn't be worse"
"Today's rhymes," They claim
"Are composed in free verse."

Free verse writers
all know how to wing it
But if you think it's a poem
Just try to sing it.

A sad state of affairs
near breaks my heart
The judges all are convinced
That free verse is art

I'm shakin' my head
Bidin' my time
Till someone figures out
A poem needs to rhyme!

Star-spangled Elegy

America, what has become of thee?
One man, one vote our motto, yet we mock it
where money silences democracy

Test scores measure kids' proficiency
while teaching them to think not on the docket
America, what has become of thee?

In fear, we forfeit civil liberties,
abide elected hands in corporate pockets
and money silences democracy

A wall, our immigration policy
Just slam the door on foreigners and lock it!
America, what has become of thee?

The war machine rolls on eternally,
its Big Wheels churning suffering into profit,
the money silencing democracy

Yet, mired in patriotic fantasy,
we raise our fist to any who would knock it
America, what has become of thee?
where money silences democracy

Joan Harris

Rest Area

Autumn's breeze rustles the trees; we cook grilled cheese at our ease. "Those smell super!" exclaims a state trooper slowing his cruiser. Across the park, in the gathering dark, chain gangs of monarchs in prison attire set a tree on fire.

How Do I Love Cheese?

How do I love cheese? Let me count the ways
I love it grilled, American on white
Schmeared on an onion bagel, toasted light
In pecan cheese balls served on holidays
Shingled with fresh fruit on party trays
Swirled in fondue pots by candlelight
I love it hard, aged cheddar with a bite
I love it soft, baked Brie with maple glaze
I love it cheese-caked, lemony and smooth
Blistered on a New York pizza slice
Macaronied into comfort food
Nachoed… patty-melted…batter-fried…
If Death disguised himself as crab Rangoon
I'd take the bait and gladly pay the price

Submerged

I'm mad for the smell of paper,
a habit I fell into of necessity
Without worry for things left undone,
I communicate only with glances

A habit I fell into of necessity,
connecting the dots into a mandala
I communicate only with glances
a balance of sweet, sour and salty

Connecting the dots into a mandala
I must turn to face my own life
a balance of sweet, sour and salty
alone with no one to guide me

I must turn to face my own life
without worry for things left undone
Alone with no one to guide me
I'm mad for the smell of paper

Creation as Told By a Third Grade Boy

On the first day God said "Let there be light!" So, there was day instead of night.

On the second day God said, "Let there be water and land, so I can dance to a band."

On the third day God made the birds in the air, so He could get them out of his hair.

On the fourth day God said, "Let there be fish in the sea, so I can catch them all for me."

On the fifth day God said, "Let there be animals everywhere, running around in their underwear."

On the sixth day God said, "Let there be man." That's why we are here.

On the seventh day He sat back and had a beer.

Doni Hartley

The Old Fiddle on the Shelf

Jerry Hartley

That old fiddle on the shelf, could tell a story or more
Of nights when three generations rolled up the rug on the
    floor.
The cook-stove held a glow so the temperature stayed just
    right
While we danced and clapped and sang songs with the
    fiddle at Gramma's Friday night.

Times were different in those days and families gathered
    together
With candle lights, and water at the pump and no regard
    for the weather.
Sometimes the winter winds outside would whistle and
    howl and blow
And bring a storm to keep you inside, away from mounting
    snow.

In summer the family would picnic, kids ran through the
    banging door
But the fiddle came out on Friday nights and they rolled up
    the rug on that floor.
When the dancing was done and the songs were all sung,
    Gramma served coffee and pie.
Then they'd roll into place that rug on the floor before
    bidding each other goodbye.

I Spy with My Little Eye

I spy with my little eye something that I hear.
I cannot see it really, so I spy it with my ear.
I spy with my little eye something soft, like sand.
I can't see it really, so I spy it with my hand.
I spy with my little eye what tastes like a cinnamon
    bun.
I can't see it really, so I spy it with my tongue.
I spy with my little eye a smell just like a rose.
I can't see it really, so I spy it with my nose.

Daylight Savings Time

Daylight savings ends today—funny but it seems
We wake up now to sunshine, disrupting pleasant dreams.
Our day gets light so early but ends with early night
Makes one think of God's first words…"Let there be light!"

Daylight savings started. Monday's dawn came late.
But the rush-hour traffic doesn't slow, knowing work won't wait.
If we go to bed by ten pm, when it is barely night,
How are we saving daylight if we sleep while it's still light?

My Song

Samantha Heffley

Love can't change the dark thoughts
It can only placate the symptoms
Or hide the tears, streams that won't
Stop the burden I've become.

Wanting my song to stop the melody to fade
So the volume will be turned down on the others who
    surround me
Giving them a respite to the noise
The beat of my heart is strong, but the strength of my
    harmony has dissipated
A whisper of notes that I want to harmonize

Yet the volume button is broken
The song that is my life contains
flats and sharps at random intervals
Controlling the tempo seems impossible
Enjoying the melody isn't in the cards
All I'm doing is following along on repeat,
At this point it's just a broken treble clef.

Fighting for Normalcy

Compulsions, ticks, tremors
Comprise myself.
Symptoms with no relief
Which are there for life.

Anxiety plagues
My daily thoughts and actions
So I can never
Reach a sense of calm

Depression grips hold of
My heart and mind
Rendering me useless
With a burden resting on my chest

Bipolar disorder swings
like a pendulum inside
My head causing severe UPS
Followed by tremendous DOWNS.

I, myself have all of these
Yet they do not define me
Nor do they reflect my
Sanity or Insanity

I am who I am because
Of these diseases that I carry
Some parts are good
And others not so much.

Fighting for normalcy
Is what I do everyday
Control is an important part
In living with all these.

Especially when they are
Supposed to be controlling me
And sometimes they do
Only when I lose my normalcy.

Inside the Walls

The majesty of the clouds
And the trees remind me of home
With grandparents and where
The willow trees would blow.

A scene can be created by
Peering through tree branches
A snapshot of the world
Resulting in a beautiful image

Between each tree branch
Sets a new scene to be written
A new cloud to be described or
A bird's nest that needs to be detailed

Colors of the sky, leaves, and clouds
Set up the picture as a whole
Creating one mesmerizing picture
To share for the world to appreciate

Just looking out one window
Can tell a story of a day
Painting the set of a play
Which we call life.

Brew Time

Warren Holliday

I enter
another
three minutes
of my life
on the microwave,

and watch it
tick away as
my tea heats.

The Wine Glass

I broke the last wine glass today,
It was the last of a set of six,
Crystal,
It played a tune when wet
Much to the delight of my son,
I bought it in Hartford with its brothers,
It was a gift to try and ease a caused wound,
Coming home on weekends,
Trying to earn a living by being away
    and staying home at the same time,
Tension,
Things crack like wine glasses and the pieces are
    swept up and thrown away,
Funny how some of us can cry over a broken wine
    glass.

Two Wooden Bowls

On the top of the chest of drawers they sit,
the small atop the bigger wooden bowl, oblong both,
as feathers, light material, hand carved, reminiscent of another world.
The wheels cross the distance between the asphalt and the shoulder
dust floats on the air breeding with the rays of a sunny afternoon.
A little wooden shack, miserable, piles of wooden bowls around,
slices of fresh curled wood, like snowflakes fill the floor
crawling around unfinished bowls, as chicks around their mother.
Behind the shack, the mountains spread their perfume
a river crosses down at the valley. Then we see the man.
Dark thick hair, shy, awkward gesture from artistic hands
an Indian-European model for Velasquez light darkness drama.
The lines in his face, his aquiline nose, black eyeballs lowered,
thick eyebrows defend him from the look of strangers.
His lightly curved back anatomically prepared to accept the chore,
the chisel born in these callous industrious hands of his.
Bony volumes in his stretched tanned body forms a sculpture
the fabric carves its texture in dirty lines and swirls across the volumes.
He could have been a Ramses, his strong profile defying the horizon,
he was the man who simply carved light pieces of wood. Simple.
No majestic Ramseic sandals stepping on the dry soil, no stony pectoral,
just the curved backed rough being, no more than what he was. Simple.

Mila Kette

The sound of car doors slamming, words, dirty children's silhouettes,
a pile of fresh carved bowls holds the air around them
exhibiting their light rough skin, tempting, pale, primitive, pure.
The man's hands are dirty, dark. He is not literate.
He doesn't know he's an artist or where America is
he just sits and carves wooden bowls;
art flows from his hands as water from the spring down to the valley.
The artist is a man who doesn't know what an artist means.
The man, the artist, needs to feed his children.

Two wooden bowls sit on my lap as the car gains distance.
I feel as if I carry this man's children and I speak softly
only they can hear my whispering "there, there."
Only they can hear the man's, the artist's thoughts they carry.
They will go to a far land, they will cross rivers and mountains,
there, where the sun shines in different angles,
there, where the words have different meanings and tastes.
The two wooden bowls will sit inside each other as if they speak
and finally they will both find comfort in their oblong, concave contact,
and they will look for acceptance from the chest drawer,
there, where they can't understand the language spoken.

Ebony

Her eyes were gazing
at the stars in her hand,
the left no less
the hand of the heart
where she kept her love;
the bills he sent her
as sure as life and she paid
with sighs and tears.
Teeth brushed to perfection
handkerchief held firmly
against crying luscious lips.
From the tropical ebony face
a glassy tear lazily slipped,
fell to the soil
a discarded flower.

Lil' Boat and Sky

Lil' boat where are you now
Lil' boat, that I'm still here
That the waters passed by
And I'm looking at the sky?
So much water, so lil' time
So many fish swimming flying clouds.
Water closing around your womb
Warm water cold sky.
Lil' boat my passion waits
Lil' boat for your come back.
Do you feel the waves caressing
The wood you're made of
The trees you once were
The leaves that fell and are gone?
I found love and warmth and dry land
But you're floating alone somewhere
In silence, quietly sinking
Taking my glance, the nerves, the skin
Away.

Cottage Life

Stephanie Kramer

Since Saturday at 5:00
I have been residing
In a cozy cottage,
Feeling as if I have
Always lived here.
I feel my being relaxing.
I am stimulated by
The color,
  Shapes,
    Sounds,
      Silence
And the opportunity for laziness
That the "seaside" offers freely.
Come bedtime, the lake's waves
Make themselves audible
For the insomniac.
But...it is now afternoon.
The Doves, Robins and Peter Rabbit encourage
Me...to paint the beauty outside my peaceful porch.
Inside I am smiling.

Surprises

green in the snow
a touch of color in the white frosted world
a touch of hope in a evil place
a touch of god in hell

Samantha Kate Laffay

Experience

experience
broken hearts, crushed dreams, broken fantasies
sad somber melodies
funerals, tough decisions, opposite visions
head on collisions
and vacations to the dead sea

What's My Line

Where is a sinner a winner
But a saint, ain't.

That ain't no justice,
Makes me faint.

To dream for rightness
Seems so quaint.
We live in a time of taint.

William Lucht

Don McGee

On Christmas Eve

A young boy and girl huddled together
For warmth against winter's bitter weather
With tattered old clothing and worn-out shoes
These two children had nothing else to lose
On Christmas Eve

Battered and abused forced them to take flight
From a broken home not treating them right
The two crouched on a heated sidewalk grate
Wrapped up in plastic so heat wouldn't escape
On Christmas Eve

Shoppers avoid them with hardly a stare
As they stepped around them without a care
Hurrying about for last minute gifts
Time was running out to complete their lists
On Christmas Eve

Suddenly a man appeared by their side
Whose voice was friendly and smile was wide
"Come gather round me, you're my guests tonight
In the restaurant over by that light"
On Christmas Eve

The children could hardly believe their ears
Their hearts filled with joy and their eyes with tears
They quickly stood up and embraced the man
And walked across the street holding his hand
On Christmas Eve

He led them into a fine dining place
With white table cloths of linen and lace
A table reserved for them by the door
It didn't seem to matter that they were poor
On Christmas Eve

His clothing was old and worn out like theirs
No one in the dining room seemed to care
The staff catered to their every request
Treating them all as very special guests
On Christmas Eve

There was plenty of food and laughter too
Even hot chocolate on the menu
They ate until they couldn't eat any more
The staff all waved as they went out the door
On Christmas Eve

The children smiled and thanked the stranger
Hoping that their time with him would linger
He surprised them by asking with a smile
"Will you walk with me for just awhile?
On Christmas Eve

"I have some good friends who live out this way
They promised to give you a place to stay
They have big hearts and a wonderful home
I'm sure you'd prefer it to being alone"
On Christmas Eve

The man and woman greeted them warmly
Their smiles were especially friendly
"You two must be cold and very tired
Please warm yourself by the roaring fire"
On Christmas Eve

Two cats and a dog soon joined everyone
The children played with them and had lots of fun
The stranger hugged them all and said goodbye
The boy and the girl had tears in their eyes
On Christmas Eve

The stranger knew that his job was not done
His life's whole purpose had not just begun
Thousands of years ago and ever since
Mary gave birth to a Heavenly Prince
On Christmas Eve

May Jesus bless you this most Holy Night
When God gave His Son as a Shining Light
To show us the path to His Father's Door
And give us salvation forevermore
On Christmas Eve

Memorial Day Tribute

What is this hallowed place upon which we now stand
Where thousands of white crosses seem to dot the land

We are told that here lay the souls of heroes past
Who gave their lives so America's peace will last

The hundreds of thousands throughout our short history
Who shed their blood to ensure lasting victory

They protected our homes from the horrors of war
While taking the fight to our enemy's shore

The sacrifices were many from this great cast
Whose voices now silenced but their deeds everlast

Who were these fearless warriors who are laid at rest
We cannot forget them or their courageous quest

We place the American Flag at each white cross
Reciting their rank and name to honor their loss
On Memorial Day

On Sleeping

Loretta Majoy

I love to go to sleep at night,
It's then my weary soul takes flight
To distant places in my mind.

I might have a key and walk the hall
My choice of doors may make me fall…but…
It's just a dream and I won't die.
Who knows? Behind *that* door I'll fly.

One door stands open and beckons me
I see two men—or is it three?
I'm curious, but I take my time,
For it may be just a pantomime.

I wander through more doors and then
I see myself go through again
The one I tried and hurried out
One I thought I'd do without

I see there lovers from my past
This time the pain and hurt won't last.
The beauty of the dream is this:
There's no future wrapped up in the kiss

My journey continues and I don't tire;
I forget all else; it's my desire
To join the dream people and make them see
How much they are amusing me.

Too bad…the time goes rushing by
And soon the scenes racing past my eye
Fade quickly into the morning sun,
Leaving feelings and images much undone.

Say No To A Fat Cat

My cat watches me each time I head for the door
And makes a fuss though she doesn't care where I stray,
Just so her dish which sits squarely on the floor
Won't be empty today.

I've thought of just serving her up a buffet
Of tuna and salmon and other treats she'll adore.
If I do that, though, she might soon outweigh

An acceptable cat size and then oh, what a chore
To put a cat on a diet. No, I give in, I'll obey—
Play our game and of course her dish just as before
Won't be empty today.

For Mario

You opened some of the windows of
your soul and drew me in.

You shared your past and helped me
see where you have been.

Your hurt shows through, your mask
can't hide the pain my friend

Your feelings don't surface for you
have made them yours alone to tend.

What will you be like in a week or
two if you don't change how you
feel about you.

What will you be like in a year or
two when you are used to the pain
and it's used to you.

Bruce Molnar

Migizi Yabwen Eagle Dreamer

I feel very blessed to visualize a soaring Eagle when I dream. A most regal and majestic raptor.

When observed in flight at a perfect angle from Mother Earth- the sight of the Eagle projects a snowy-white, diamond-like brilliance that emanates from its head and tail plumes.

Soaring and ascending, spiraling in the sky—just as if it were dancing in a ceremonial ritual.

Every day the Eagle soars to great heights in Father Sky— over vast distances at astounding speeds.

Climbing, turning, searching, and sailing along with pure grace and natural beauty.

It seems that Eagles truly appreciate their strength, independence, and freedom.

Gliding and descending—all the while searching the terrain for prey to dive upon and snatch up, while carefully evading potential hazards so the Eagle can journey safely back to its aerie.

Eagles cannot only choose to fly in the calm and bright blue skies of the day.

Eagles must fly to survive, soaring to hunt prey successfully to provide for their young eagles, before they provide for themselves.

The Eagle takes from Mother Earth only what is needed to care for its family and to stay alive, keeping strong to be able to fly and soar again.

The Eagle you see is a servant and a part of the Creator's lifecycle.

The Eagle is not thwarted by adversity but is fearless and determined in its purpose.

The beauty of what the Eagle sees and knows will never be understood by the *Anishinabek* or any *Pe'matse'juk* (living people). But only by its Creator -the one the *Bodewadmik* know as *Kshe'mnIto*, the Great Spirit, God!

Look to the Eagle for the many lessons it can teach all of us about life's joys and struggles and give thanks to *Kshe'mnIto* (Great Spirit) for the gift of the majestic and magnificent Eagle (*Migizi*).

Ahow— amen

My Pond

Robert Reynolds

My flowers share their beauty
as they smile upon the sun.
Petals are bold in color,
with tear drops of summer rain.

I am consumed by a gentle spirit,
perhaps a fragrance of liberty.
The stillness of a summer pond
is music to my ears.

Birds are my loyal critics,
with soft sounds of approval.
I shall not be part of politics
or policies of shame.

My foundations are the purity
of simple existence,
regardless of historic habits.
This shall form my way of life.

To receive water and fish from the pond,
other food from God's earth.
This will give me great satisfaction.
My mind will be energized.

There is little concern about my meals.
I am not swayed by fermented desires,
nor shall I make a tailor wealthy,
my clothes are limited, though adequate.

The joy of reading by a fireside
brings peace at the end of a day.
Night noises and winds in the tree tops
will bring comfort in my hours of rest.

From the sweet music of the stars
will come the passion of heaven.
It is the sky, earth and trees
that make a day so beautiful.

I heard an owl call out to a mate,
watched a robin make a nest.
A fox nurturing her young pups
in the hollow of a hillside lair.

There is no longer labor to pay taxes
for the creation of useless things.
Nor do I spend with the grocer
when I can grow food in the soil.

There is no obedience to laws
that alienate my given rights.
It is time to put my boat in the pond,
to fish for my next meal.

I will sit quietly as evening
spreads across still waters,
with a sunset in the western sky.
I am eager for the arrival of tomorrow.

Walking in the Woods

In the windy air I saw a red hawk.
He found his meals with winging stalk.

From high above, in wane of a day,
he would gently glide for moving prey.

Darting creatures in my walking path,
fell sudden victim to hungry wrath.

I heard a sound rise in late evening skies,
then quiet wings for another try.

By then my walk was loudly heard,
squirrels found height with chirping birds.

I walked through beds of gentle ferns,
where mossy rocks caused pools to churn.

Darting fish played hide and seek,
while sun drenched leaves made me peek.

Glowing light from sunset skies,
brought heavenly visions to my eyes.

An army of color descending from God,
to bless earth's kingdoms, though it was odd.

Some preferred darkness, in a quiet plain.
Shadows gave cover to birds in the lane.

In Muir Wood Forest, a whispered song,
creations of nature are forever gone.

Death of creatures will balance life's spear.
This harmony of nature cannot bring fear.

Hawk and the mouse may be long gone,
yet forest and nature shall always live on.

My walk has ended with a sunset sky,
leaving God's Castles with a grateful good-bye.

Hiker

I took a walk.

It went on forever and was over too soon
Recharging batteries I never knew I had

I'm so alive and sleep like a dead man
Deserts in bloom, fields of gold,
An infinity of stars, the scars of firestorms.
I fly through mountains and ford rivers,
The ridge crests are endless.
Water carving and caressing the landscapes,
I trudge the definition of majesty and grandeur.
Bring it! Brothers and sisters on quests of their own.
I'm proud of my country and all its gracious people
Strangers opening their hearts and arms to strangers.
The way it's supposed to be.

Roller coasters of emotion sweep me daily;

Exhaustion, euphoria, loneliness, achievement, desolation
The feelings are overwhelming and I turn to cry.
Can it be just me?
A hard body, incredibly fragile.
My cup is full, so amazingly blessed
I made the time.

I took a walk.

David Rolsten

Rustlings

Listen! Listen closely…hear the
rustlings of the leaves in the tree tops;
faint, but clear as the soft breeze
pushes leaf against leaf,
leaving branches and trunks still.

The sound is gentle, soothing as
if to foreshadow kindness and respect.
The breeze is high, caressing only the
tops of the tall oaks; I feel no movement
on my skin where I stand.

Should Greek mythology be true,
that the rustlings in the leaves of
the tall oak trees is a sign from the Gods,
then today is going to be a good day;
a joyous and perhaps prosperous one.

There is no violence or anger in
the dance of these leaves;
no sharp pitching of branches and trunks
turning and twisting as if to be
splintered and broken by a strong force.

This leaf talk invites me to sit, look and listen;
enjoy the squirrel sitting upright on a limb,
watch butterflies flutter in follow the leader mode,
smell fresh cut grass from my neighbor's lawn,
and taste the tart lemonade as it quenches my thirst.

Oh leaves, speak to me and I will listen.
Soft breezes, sing to me and my heart will dance.

Ronald M. Ruble

Even-Keeled

Ah, the delight of being on a true course,
leveled, running through smooth
water or gliding across ice on skates;
soft breezes filtering through my hair.
The serenity of that feeling cradles me.

All my life that is the course I preferred,
easy as resting on my back
soaking up the noonday sun;
muscles relaxed and mind at peace.
"Not a care in the world," my grandpa would say.

My life has not been on a straight line.
Full of ups and downs, happy and sad,
excitement and boredom, successes and failures,
choices made well and those better not made,
cares that kept me up at night.

I work to stay focused, not to list side to side
except now and then when it feels right.
Some choices lean toward the conservative
while other choices reflect the liberal.
Too often, there is no middle ground on which to
walk.

As I age, I realize the need to be sound
physically, mentally, and spiritually.
My family, friends and faith have provided the
strength, love, compassion, and order to
keep me from crashing, sinking, spiraling
into depths where I feel in limbo, lost,
swallowed by darkness.

When Innocence Flavored the Air

Childhood memories
flood my awareness,
take me to places of joy.
Times when language
was less harsh,
intent honorable,
touch gentle,
laughter often,
hurt accidental,
when hugs and kisses
soothed my pain.
A time when future
had a naive understanding,
when innocence
flavored the air.
Initials were carved into trees,
with dates, hearts, arrows;
kooky references of the times.
Snorted laughter, joyful giggles,
unbridled squeals of delight
echoed across the landscape;
coursed down the valley
as did the river at its base.
Normally outside, not inside,
our social conversation fused
with each part of the day.
When wonder abounded,
reached out to embrace discovery.
I long for those times again.

Honor Them

Row upon row of headstones
and stars and stripes of red, white, and blue.
I am son, brother, uncle, father, grandfather
and great-grandfather, because they lay there.

Our freedoms and independence have come with
the costs of losing arms, legs, lives; of digging graves.
Still, we fight for freedom every day
with too many men and women lost.

They gave all when there was
nothing more for them to give.
Their service and sacrifices
should never be forgotten.

Children should learn about the
importance of war memorials.
For when we forget our history, we
lose sight of the cost of our independence.

Pay tribute to the memories
of the deserving, heroic, gallant.
Stop! Listen to the beats of your heart.
Our beats are here, because they rest there.

Bottle o' what?

Joel D. Rudinger

A bottle of water, a bottle of wine,
chardonnay, pinot, merlot are all fine.
A bottle of ketchup, a bottle of juice,
bottled up fears being chased by a moose.
Bottled up feelings, so sad and so blue,
you'd think your ass was a bottle of glue.
A bottle of rum plus a bottle of coke
makes for a drink so sweet that you'll choke.
A bottle for grandpa, a bottle for babe,
As Humpty told Alice, "the mome raths outgrabe."
Bottoms up means bottle raised to the sky.
Bottoms down means you raised it too high.

Our Life Is A Dance to A Song We Cannot Hear

There is a vibration in the air. Do you feel it?
Sometimes it is soft and gentle like a silent harp.
Sometimes it is violent enough to shake my teeth.
I feel It and It feels me.

You and I, we move as one,
turning to the left or to the right.
We work and love and cry and age
as we, untamed, dance on upon Earth's thin crust
as it and we plummet and spin
through never empty, never ending space.

What is this ghost vibration in the air?
What controls the beat and rhythm of my heart?
What releases the channels of my mind
when mind and spirit merge as one?

Does the song I sing reflect the rhythm of a larger breath?
When I lead, is my dance of life a mere illusion?
When I am led, the dance itself becomes the master of my thoughts.

A silent singing directs our feet,
brings together purpose and potential,
decides whether our feet go tap-tippy-tap in happy time
or drag along with aching legs of stone.

What moves us all to play *hide-and-seek*
or *tag-you're-it* in the blazing sun?
What makes a shadowy song of night seem safe one day
but on the next a cloud of terror?

Our life is a dance to a song we cannot hear.
What rhythm drove me away from home when I was young?
What silent sound has brought me back?

When Winds Blow Me

When winds blow me around the edges of buildings,
   past dark trunks of autumn trees,
     I dance in joy and wonder.
       I am going somewhere new,
         away from sisters, brothers, family, friends,
        away from everything familiar.
        Adventure calls! Adventure!
       Blow on, sweet breezes.
      Take *me* with you.
        Life is short enough.

Every Song Comes to An End

Every road, desert, shoreline, mountain range, and river has an end.
Every song or dance, poem or story begins and ends to bless the spirit.
Every painting and sculpture begins and ends with inspiration.

Each day begins as the sun comes up in the east.
For a brief while, the sky is bright,
then day ends as the light sinks down glowing in the west.

I am conceived in love, born a child, grow into adulthood,
learn to work and play and harmonize with friends, then grow old.
All life arrives at its predictable end.

Endings are beautiful

The Technological Struggle

Domenic Sberna

It is a driving force
And a major downfall

Running our lives, inside and out
Pulling the strings, to our existence.

Growing, feeding, thriving
Depending, forgetting, denying

The products are growing
Thus controlling our lives

The growing is feeding
This constant usage need

The thriving is killing
The utter hope of humanity

The dependence is bringing
The downfall of mankind

Forgettance is unbeknownst to us
In the mechanical crankshaft of our brains

Denial is who we are
It is in our nature

Technology of man
Destroyer of the human race

But only, if we let it become thus
Only, if we do not control ourselves

Before the machines, control our existence.

A Better Outlook

This world is a great place
So, even if you fall from grace
You still have time to find your place

Look on the bright side of life
Don't go looking for a strife

Yes, hardships will come your way
But, that doesn't mean that they will stay

For life is fleeting
And we are all just needing

A friend, a companion
A pick me up, a new outlook

Enjoy your time alive
Because one day, we all die

That day is not now
So, when you ask me how

I tell you to go
Go and do good

Be happy
Be kind

And most importantly
Be positive
And be the change you wish to see!

Hope

Hope

There is always hope

Hands at your throat
The end of the rope

There is still hope

Never give up
Never stop fighting
The light is still guiding

Today, you cannot cope
You still have hope

The mountain's slope
Is keeping you down

At the bottom, you are weary
Weary, anxious, and hopeful

You can overcome
Just as others have before

Never give up
Never give in

For as long as you're still breathing
You have hope

Some days that is everything
Some days it is all you have

Hope.

Come Summer

Linda Simmons

The school bus stops on the curve of the road,
by the big oak tree we're the last of its load.
My older brother, my big sister and me,
all hop off with delight and glee.

The school year is over, the homework is done,
it's time for summer and lots of fun.
I cross the road and look up to see our big white farm
  house waiting for me.
I skip, I hop, I jump on a rock and look down to see,
a little red lady bug has landed on me.
Away it flies as it shoots to the sky with wings
  as strong as can be.
The sun is warm as I run thru the grass,
I twirl around dizzy and fall, what a blast!
I'm as happy as a lark on this beautiful day,
look my friends are coming it's time to play.
We jump from the porch, play a game of tag,
hide-n-seek is silly and we laugh till we sag.
Oh the days of summer are happy for me,
I'll be young a little longer and that's just ok with me.

Rob Smith

In all the land there were no women so beautiful as Job's daughters; and their father gave them an inheritance along with their brothers.
(Job 42:15)

Kesiah*

Cinnamon came bundled in hope
as a baby should,
with parents dreaming to make
her inheritance softer than
their African slave-flesh.
Her skin so lightly brown that
someone would love her,
someone with a last name,
someone who owned only himself.
Er kam aus deutschland,
He came from Germany
till death they didn't part;
their children crossing to a place
where Quakers practiced a safer abolition.

I like to think she sang
to her twelve children
as my mother sang,
in a language understood by love,
not measured in syllables.

I am so white,
ask anyone who knows me,
99.5% European by measured count.
Still, the heir of cinnamon, child of Kesiah,
and she marks my skin every summer
being reborn in the warmth of a new day.

*Heb: *cinnamon*

Sister

When mother went away
to care for the baby,
sister took charge.
It was the way it had to be
with little brothers, and
mother being so soon
gone.
Father was busy
working numbers,
but seeing only dead ends.
Strong children rise
to needs unspoken knowing
that at the center of a house is a place
to run when dreams
turn dark,
or teacher says "Everyone, remember
to take your pictures home,
the ones you made for your mothers."
Such a simple thing,
but she went away to care for the baby never seen,
and school art was loaded into a dresser drawer
till sister would bring out her
drawings to lay
side by side
in a children's gallery
seen by no adult eyes.
It was the best she could arrange.
It was the way it had to be
with mother so far away.

Keeping House

Half of Dad's paycheck went to a housekeeper,
a woman to keep house and be home
when the three of us walked back from school.
Hers was the bedroom where
Poppy and Nana stayed in happier days.

Evenings and weekends off,
— most didn't last long—
we being the default excuse—
though always striving to be good,
not wishing a father's despair.

Some lasted longer.

Winky, my sister's favorite,
nineteen and pretty—Jehovah's Witness, though,
and my father raged on a Thursday when work held him
    over,
and she took us to a meeting.
He wasn't bothered that her husband was in prison for
    refusing Korea,
but then, his nephew, Ralph, spent World War II in
    Leavenworth.
(I was well past forty when Ralph told me that he loved my
    mother,
she being the only welcoming one after release.
When he told me, I envied that he had even one memory
    of her.)

Mary MacDonald liked it when my brother and I
sat on her lap and she'd press us against her breasts.
Her son, Malcolm, always took my little brother to the
    basement to shoot an air rifle.
In later years, my sister called her abusive—we thought it
    love.

For a short time,
we had a black housekeeper, her name not remembered,
    but I loved her.
One memory sticks:
She called me in from outside (playing outside never caused
    trouble)
—time to get dressed for afternoon kindergarten,
on a hanger, a perfectly pressed white dress shirt.
Nobody had done that before.
I loved her for that, but she lasted less than a month—
boyfriends came to visit and took our bed linens.
Daddy couldn't afford to buy new ones.

Seasonal Inflation

At night, in the flood of spotlights
Santa and Rudolph gather around a snowman
in the neighbor's yard.

They look so plump and full,
dancing in the winter wind,
such brightly colored bags of air heralding Christmas,
or something.

Jesus is not there.

I'm glad the Virgin Mary
isn't there with a peasant face
bloated like a gourd, or Joseph
whose lantern wouldn't hold a candle
to the greater wattage of power.

Tomorrow their vinyl bodies will lie
puddled in the killing fields
of an otherwise neat landscape.
Just so many lifeless forms
waiting for the landfill.

Jesus is not there.

Mary and Joseph fled to Egypt in the night.
Hiding among the other refugees,
and not among the forms to rise
this night when the electric blowers are plugged in.

Colette Sommer Steuk

Frogs

Frogs leap and leap everywhere,
getting ready to hibernate for winter.
Frogs must go
Under the mud and away from the cold.
Winter is coming too fast.

The Day is Done

The hill, small as can be.
The birds sing, as calm as can be.
People wear hats
and play with a friendly cat
on a hot summer day.

As slowly the day comes to an end.
The joyful day is done.
Night is coming.
How dark it can be.

People sleeping in warm beds.
Dreaming as a gleeful heart can be.
What a happy day it will be tomorrow!

Poem

Poem, sweet poem
I like to write my thoughts each day
Tell me what to say
I know this is the end of day
I wish I knew
what to say

A poem based on Anne Morrow Lindbergh's meditations in "Gift from the Sea"

Inner Eye

Dana Sandberg Vargo

Distractions, so many…
how to remain whole
when stretched thin;
family, husband, children,
home, work, friends.
Overburdened. Overwhelmed.
A balance, is it achievable
in this life of multiplicity?

Energy perpetually spent,
drained away.
Contemplation
desirable, yet distant.
How can we nurture the soul,
our core, our inner eye,
in the midst of distractions
so many…?

Oft torn from center,
removed from self.
Depleted, peace eluded
among myriad pulls.
Be still. Contemplate. Read.
Be creative. Reflect. Pray.
Take time to nourish the soul.
Reclaim your true essence.

Practice the art of solitude to
find joy in the now.
Practice the art of solitude to
find peace in the here.
Redeem your inner strength.
Rediscover your inner eye.
Find again
the love in me and thee.

The Plan

Sandra Wright

I've been thinking ahead
to the time when I'm dead.
Do I want a grand show
when it's my time to go?
Should I be fixed up and buried
or cremated and carried
to a place to be scattered
to a place that once mattered.
I'll float on the breeze
toward the lake and the trees.
The decision is made
no funeral parade.
Just a simple goodbye
When it's my time to die.

For Alex

Why is Fate so cruel
To those who are needed by so many?
Uncaring,
It scratches at the eyes of those
Who see the straightest.
It tears down brilliant minds
Reducing them to the absurd.
It snaps the strongest between its fingers
Crushing them to dust in time.
Leaving strewn in its path
The history of mankind

Summer Night

Soft cricket songs
Tickle my ears.
Fireflies flicker
Hypnotizing me
I am lulled to sleep
Swaying in my hammock
Under the stars.

Index of Poets

Gerald (Jerry) Bauer has lived in Huron for twenty years. He is a retired Lutheran pastor who served churches in Michigan, Wisconsin, and Ohio. He's published six chapbooks of scripture poems and sees poetry as an avenue of creative expression.

Robert P. Boehk is a lifelong Ohio resident, and has been married to Laurie for thirty-five years with three adult children and four beautiful grandchildren. In 2016 Bob retired from the practice of law after a more than thirty-year career as a construction attorney.

Nancy Brady is a lifelong native of Ohio, who has lived in Huron since 2005. Her primary focus is writing haiku. Before her retirement, she often found inspiration on her treks back and forth to work as a pharmacist. She has been writing poetry since high school and states, "Writing poems is one way for all people to express their emotions and experiences."

Eileen Wikel Darby writes that poetry is her lifeline to a happy, creative life. She finds joy in reading the work of others and in writing her own.

Jennie Mae Fish Jennie Mae Fish is a retired teacher who has lived in Huron for fourteen years. She has always loved words, books, and libraries. Passionate about reading, traveling, and swimming, she also enjoys playing with watercolors.

Bill Gassett describes himself as a preacher, poet, and painter. He is the director of Crescendo Ministries. He and his wife, Donna, have lived in Huron for more that twenty-five years. They have one daughter and two granddaughters. He sees his poetry as a vital expression of his faith and his love for people.

Donna Gassett writes with emotional sensitivity. This is her first year for submitting poems for 44839. "Rose in the Cradle" was awarded third place honors.

Will Gravitt is a college administrator, an occasional poet, and a fan of the use of words to make the world a better place. He is happy to call Huron home since June of 2019.

Gary Harmon has lived in Huron for fifty years. He is an avid writer, and in 2017, his novel, *The Broken Spur* was published. He is a storyteller through and through. With all his writing, he is enthralled by the writers who give us the 'less than perfect.' Poets like Ogden Nash, Robert Service, Hank Williams, and Dolly Parton honor the scalawags of the world. He has enjoyed tears and laughter together for a very long time.

Joan Harris lived most of her life in the small town of Yellow Springs, Ohio. She and her husband moved to Huron six months ago to be closer to their families. A retired nurse and a sporadic poetry submitter with a varied resume, she's been published in several small magazines and an anthology, had her work read on the radio, and won the Literal Latte's food poetry contest in 2017. She gravitates toward form and rhyme (likely due to an overdose of Dr. Seuss in early childhood). She shares a creaky old house with a curmudgeon-in-training, two senior pound pups, and an orange tomcat named Peaches. (Editor's note: It has just been announced that Joan is the 2020 winner of the *Erma Bombeck Writing Competition* in the local humor category.)

Jerry Rogers Hartley's interest in journalism began as the editor of her high school yearbook. She was awarded a summer scholarship to a writer's workshop at Ohio University. That background sparked a continuing interest in writing. In 1967, she married and moved to Huron where her five children spent their school years. She now focuses on writing biographies. Her first was published in 1995; *Born in Greece, Made in America* is the story of Nick Hoty. With her entries is included a poem written by her now adult son, **Doni Hartley**, when he was in the third grade.

Samantha Heffley lives and works in Huron. Thanks to her rather public role at the post office, she has become one of the more easily recognized people in the city. Sam's been writing poetry for more than ten years and found it to be a very therapeutic means of self-expression.

Warren Holliday is a retired Regional Director for the New York State office of Parks, Recreation, and Historic Preservation. He was born, raised, and educated in the Albany, New York area. He currently lives in Huron, Ohio and enjoys traveling, Native American History, and feeding the birds.

Mila Kette has lived in the U.S. twenty-three years, twenty-one of them in Huron. She feels that writing poetry is a way to look at ordinary things and find what no one else sees in them. This is what she sees as the essence of poetry.

Jill Kinser is a long-time Ohio resident. New to the Huron area, she is loving the lake life. Jill is intrigued by poetry's ability to express emotion and story in a succinct and unique voice. She reads poetry every day, and occasionally takes a stab at writing her own.

Samantha Kate Laffay attends McCormick Junior High School and is active in softball and basketball. She has always enjoyed creative writing and has a self-published book already in the stacks of Huron Public Library. She discovered her love of poetry through her school work and has been writing poems the last couple of years. This is her first public reading of her poetry.

Bill Lucht grew up in Huron and returned with his wife, Sue, after retirement. His interest in poetry was cultivated as a child and was renewed after attending a reading held at the Presbyterian Church in Huron. Poetry has become a way of expressing life through the senses of sight, sound, touch, and emotion.

Stephanie Kramer is from the Cleveland area, but has resided in Huron over the past ten years. Her background is in performing arts as a singer and actress, and those same creative impulses flow through her writing and painting! She says with enthusiasm, "My life is filled with flowers, music, literature, nature, and art. It is all poetry!"

Don McGee is the author of three self-published books and numerous inspirational poems. Don retired from General Motors and Electronic Data Systems as an Information Technology manager and consultant. Don is also a veteran of the USAF. He and his wife, Karen, enjoy traveling and visiting with family.

Loretta M. Majoy has lived in Huron since 1994 and lives in the house that was her family's cottage for years. She always believed that she would end up living in Huron because she loved the city so much. Poetry has always been a part of her life. Whether reading or writing, poetry has provided the means of tempering the woes of being a teenager, and easing the responsibilities of being a young adult. For her, it continues to be an important outlet.

Bruce Molnar is a long-time resident of Huron. His poem "Migizi Yabwen" was first published in the June 2017 tribal publication of *Pokégnek Yajdanawa* (The Pokagons Tell It). Molnar is an enrolled tribal citizen of the Pokagon Band of Potawatomi Indians of Michigan and Indiana.

In 2018, **Robert Reynolds** was selected to be Huron's fifth Poet Laureate. He's a NE Ohio native who spent a career travelling the Great Lakes as an officer in the Merchant Marine. When the sailor returned from the sea, he settled in his favorite port of call, Huron. Here, Bob and Shirley raised their family. His appointment as laureate stems from his use of poetry at civic events, and his Occasional Poems have become a meaningful part of the city's Memorial Day observances.

David Rolsten is retired after thirty-five years of practicing dentistry, and now lives full time in what was his Huron vacation home. He considers himself blessed for the opportunity to experience a lot of life adventures which range from putting himself through school to mountain climbing on peaks such as Mt Ranier. In 2016, he hiked the Appalachian Trail, and in 2019 walked the Pacific Crest Trail.

Ronald M. Ruble has lived in Huron since 1970. Here, he raised two sons (Eric and Kristofer) who graduated from Huron High School and later BGSU. He has received recognition and awards for his work as a playwright, poet, and fiction writer. He is the author of two volumes of poetry, *The Pulse of Life* and *Words Walk*. From 2011-2014, he served as Huron's Poet Laureate. He enjoys poetry because it centers on the use of words and leads to places where minds, imaginations, and creativity thrive.

Joel D. Rudinger has lived in Huron for fifty-one years, and served as a professor at BGSU-Firelands from 1967 to 2012. He has creative theses in poetry from the University of Alaska (1964) as well as the University of Iowa's Writers Workshop (1966). His poetry books include *First Edition: 40 Poems, Lovers and Celebrations*, and *Symphonia Judaica*. He was Huron Poet Laureate from 2014 to 2017. He is a member of the Firelands Writing Center and the Huron Rotary Club.

Dominic Sberna is a graduate of Bowling Green State University. Originally from Bellevue, Ohio, Dominic is a photographer, who enjoys literature, poetry, craft beer, traveling, and good company; especially the company of his wife, Kaitlyn. Poetry is something that can bind all walks of life together, and can truly convey insight, in just a few words.

Linda Simmons has a love for words. Through them she tries to capture and convey the depth of the human existence in ways which are fascinating and fun.

Rob Smith grew up in NE Ohio, but his career took him to Pennsylvania, New Jersey, and southern Ohio. In 2005, he moved to Huron to finish his novels and write poetry. In 2006, he won the Robert Frost Poetry Award, and was Huron's Poet Laureate from 2009-2011. Three of his works, *The Immigrant's House* (poetry), *McGowan's Call,* and *Sand Dollar Island* (novels) are catalogued in the Library of Congress.

Colette Sommer Steuk, age 11, is a fifth grader at Woodlands Intermediate School. She enjoys poetry, art, crafts, and participates in soccer and running club. Colette plays the piano and flute, and is an active member of the Huron Library's Girls that Code.

Dana Sandberg Vargo was born in Rochester, NY and lives in North Royalton *and* Huron, OH (where she and her husband hope to retire). She is a wife, mother, full-time paralegal, and interior designer. An avid reader, she also enjoys walking on sandy beaches, watching movies, listening to music, and attending literature readings. She writes: "It is my belief that poetry lightens the heart and brightens the world."

Sandra Wright, originally from Chicago, lives in Huron with her husband Gene. She began writing poetry at an early age and continues to enjoy the challenge of putting words together to capture a moment in time, much like her photographs.

> *About the Contest
> and the
> Judges*

Judging a poetry contest can be a daunting task. So much depends on the knowledge and preferences of the judge or judges. In an effort to provide a fair contest which would encourage all our poets to keep writing, this competition relied on a panel of people representative of our area. When the Huron Public Library teamed up with Drinian Press, the goal was to have a blindly and fairly judged outcome. Five jurors were selected. Each was presented with a packet of poems with all identifying clues of authorship removed. Each poem was read aloud and the judges were asked to assess the impact of the verse at first hearing. Afterward, and without consultation, the judges independently scored each poem on three additional rubrics (form, poetic language, and mechanics). When completed, the scores of all five judges were averaged. Every poem submitted was processed through this scrutiny. In the end, the winning poems were not selected by any one person, but by the combined judgment of this jury. Here it must be noted that not all submissions were considered for the monetary awards. Former poets laureate, members of the jury, and principals of Drinian Press were excluded from winning, but evaluated for inclusion in this volume. This was intentionally done to provide the reader with the whole range of literary voices that spring from a zip code, 44839.

Alea Dahnke has a Bachelor's and Master's degree in Spanish from Ohio Wesleyan University and Middlebury College in Vermont respectively. She has been a Spanish instructor at Sandusky High School, Huron High School, and Firelands College, BGSU. She was also a sponsor of high school international exchange student programs at SHS and HHS. She is an emeritus member of the Huron Library Board of Trustees. Her interests include foreign travel, reading, music, culinary arts, and other lifelong learning pursuits.

Vikki Morrow-Ritchie became the Director of the Huron Public Library in the fall of 2018. She took the position after serving as the Director of the Monroeville Public Library. The Cleveland area native attended the University of Toledo where she achieved both a BA and MA Degree. In addition, she holds a certification as an Ohio Public Librarian issued by the Ohio Library Council involving criteria such as a Masters in Library Science, continuing education and performance in a public library setting. Vikki enjoys swimming, hiking, reading (She is a librarian after all), traveling, going to live music shows, theater, and watching her daughter's Edge Club soccer games.

Ron Ruble served both on the panel of judges and as a contributing poet. His bio is listed above.

Joel Rudinger served both on the panel of judges and as a contributing poet. His bio is listed above.

Jan Carver Young was born and raised in Sandusky but has lived the past thirty-five years near Castalia with her husband Lou. She received her BS in Education from BGSU and, for most of her career, taught eighth grade English for Sandusky City Schools. In retirement, she spends her time working with the Unitarian Universalist Fellowship of the Firelands and reading and discussing books with friends, doing art and sewing projects, raising monarch butterflies and, occasionally, writing poetry.

Disclaimer:

No public funds were used on this project. Prize monies were underwritten by The Friends of the Huron Public Library and printing costs by the publisher. Any and all profits from book sales shall be applied to future library programs associated with the 44839 Poetry Contest.

CPSIA information can be obtained
at www.ICGtesting.com
Printed in the USA
FSHW012042060320
67768FS